NORTHERN EXPOSURE

Nordic means "from the north." Nordic skiing events were among the original Winter Olympic sports, appearing at every Winter Olympics since 1924.

CLASSIC AND FREE

Two skiing techniques, or styles, are used in Nordic skiing. The classic style involves moving skis back and forth, **parallel** to each other, along a grooved trail. The free technique involves a stride that is more like skating, with a side-to-side motion as the skiers push their legs out one at a time as they sprint through the snow.

BLAZING A TRAIL

All of the Nordic events at the Vancouver 2010 Olympics will be held at Whistler Olympic Park.

OLYMPICS FACT FILE

- The Olympic Games were first held in Olympia, in ancient Greece, around 3,000 years ago. They took place every four years until they were abolished in 393 A.D. A Frenchman named Pierre Coubertin (1863–1937) revived the Games, and the first modern Olympics—which featured only summer sports—were held in Athens in 1896.

- The first Olympic Winter Games were held in 1924 in Chamonix, France. The Winter Games were then held every four years except in 1940 and 1944 (because of World War II), taking place in the same year as the Summer Games, until 1992.

- The International Olympic Committee decided to stage the Summer and Winter Games in different years, so there was only a two-year gap before the next Winter Games were held in 1994. They have been held every four years from that time.

- The symbol of the Olympic Games is five interlocking colored rings. Together, they represent the union of the five regions of the world— Africa, the Americas, Asia, Europe, and Oceania (Australia and the Pacific Islands)—as athletes come together to compete in the Games.

Ski jumper Stefan Read (CAN) in the air at the 2006 Games.

INTRODUCTION TO BIATHLON

Biathlon means "the joining of two contests." Competitors combine cross-country skiing skills with precision rifle shooting. There are five events for both men and women—individual, sprint, pursuit, relay, and mass start.

Biathletes compete in the 15km mass start event at the 2006 Games.

BiATHLON, CROSS-COUNTRY, SKi JUMPiNG, AND NORDiC COMBINED

by Kylie Burns

Words that are defined in the glossary are in **bold** type the first time they appear in the text.

A table of abbreviations used for the names of countries appears on page 32.

Crabtree editor: Adrianna Morganelli
Proofreader: Crystal Sikkens
Editorial director: Kathy Middleton
**Production coordinator and
  prepress technician**: Katherine Berti
Developed for Crabtree Publishing Company by
RJF Publishing LLC (www.RJFpublishing.com)
Editor: Jacqueline Laks Gorman
Designer: Tammy West, Westgraphix LLC
Photo Researcher: Edward A. Thomas
Indexer: Nila Glikin

Photo Credits:
Associated Press: Wide World Photos: p. 7
Corbis: Andreas Gebert/epa: p. 28
Getty Images: front cover; pp. 3, 6, 8, 10, 12,
  13, 14, 20, 22, 24; AFP: p. 2, 4, 9, 11, 16,
  18, 21, 25, 26
Wikipedia: Dave O: p. 29

Cover: Ski jumper Thomas Morgenstern of Austria
soars through the air at the 2006 Winter Olympics.

CONTENTS

Library and Archives Canada Cataloguing in Publication

Burns, Kylie
    Biathlon, cross-country, ski jumping, and nordic combined /
Kylie Burns.

(Winter Olympic sports)
Includes index.
ISBN 978-0-7787-4021-6 (bound).--ISBN 978-0-7787-4040-7 (pbk.)
    1. Biathlon--Juvenile literature. 2. Cross-country ski racing--
Juvenile literature. 3. Ski jumping--Juvenile literature. 4. Winter
Olympics--Juvenile literature. I. Title. II. Series: Winter Olympic sports

GV854.315.B873 2009   j796.93'2   C2009-903209-0

Library of Congress Cataloging-in-Publication Data

Burns, Kylie.
  Biathlon, cross-country, ski jumping, and nordic combined /
Kylie Burns.
      p. cm. -- (Winter Olympic sports)
  Includes index.
  ISBN 978-0-7787-4040-7 (pbk. : alk. paper) -- ISBN 978-0-7787-
4021-6 (reinforced library binding : alk. paper)
  1. Skis and skiing--Juvenile literature. I. Title. II. Series.

GV854.315.B87 2010
796.93'2--dc22
                                        2009021490

Crabtree Publishing Company
www.crabtreebooks.com   1-800-387-7650
Printed in the USA/012010/CG20091228

Published in Canada
Crabtree Publishing
616 Welland Ave.
St. Catharines, ON
L2M 5V6

Published in the United States
Crabtree Publishing
PMB 59051
350 Fifth Avenue, 59th Floor
New York, New York 10118

Published in the United Kingdom
Crabtree Publishing
Maritime House
Basin Road North, Hove
BN41 1WR

Published in Australia
Crabtree Publishing
386 Mt. Alexander Rd.
Ascot Vale (Melbourne)
VIC 3032

OLYMPIC NORDIC SKIING EVENTS

Endurance, strength, and amazing skill—these are the abilities that Olympic competitors need to perform well in biathlon, cross-country skiing, ski jumping, and Nordic combined!

Kristina Šmigun (EST) on the cross-country course during the 2006 Winter Olympics.

BIATHLON'S BEGINNINGS

Biathlon began hundreds of years ago in **Scandinavian** countries, where soldiers were trained to carry a rifle while skiing. The soldiers had target-shooting contests to practice and improve their skills. The first Olympic men's biathlon competition was held in 1960. Women's biathlon was introduced 32 years later, in 1992.

STAY THE COURSE!

The biathlon course includes stretches of snow-covered trails interrupted by shooting ranges. The goal is to ski the course in the shortest time and hit as many targets as possible. This isn't easy. After completing a skiing stage of competition, athletes' hearts are racing and they are breathing heavily. Then, they quickly have to compose themselves and stop, aim, and shoot.

TO STAND, OR NOT TO STAND

Shooters are required to take different positions at different times in the competition. In the **prone position**, they lay on their stomachs while shooting. The "hit area" of the target is only 1.8 inches (4.5 cm) across. When shooters are in the **standing position**, the hit area is larger — 4.5 inches (11.4 cm) across.

Ole Einar Bjørndalen (NOR) takes aim during the shooting portion of the 2006 men's 20km individual biathlon.

GOOD AS GOLD

Ole Einar Bjørndalen (NOR) holds the record for being the only athlete to win four biathlon events during a single Olympics, in 2002. He also has the most biathlon medals of any man, with an amazing nine!

HANGING OUT ON AN ANTHILL

Magnar Solberg (NOR) trained for the shooting portion of the 1968 Olympic biathlon in a very unusual way — by lying on an anthill! This made him a precise shooter, and he hit every target in the men's individual competition to win the gold medal!

MORE ON BIATHLON

Biathlon events come in different lengths, from short to very long. In most events, competitors start at intervals, one at a time.

Germany's Kati Wilhelm during the cross-country portion of the 2006 women's 15km individual biathlon.

2006 OLYMPIC MEN'S MEDALISTS: 20km INDIVIDUAL: GOLD: MICHAEL GREIS (GER)
SILVER: OLE EINAR BJØRNDALEN (NOR)   BRONZE: HALVARD HANEVOLD (NOR)
10km SPRINT: GOLD: SVEN FISCHER (GER)   SILVER: HALVARD HANEVOLD (NOR)
BRONZE: FRODE ANDRESEN (NOR)
12.5km PURSUIT: GOLD: VINCENT DEFRASNE (FRA)   SILVER: OLE EINAR BJØRNDALEN (NOR)
BRONZE: SVEN FISCHER (GER)

INDIVIDUAL

The men's individual biathlon is 12.4 miles (20 km) long, and the women's individual event is 9.3 miles (15 km). Competitors ski five times around the course in a loop, stopping four times at the shooting ranges to shoot. A one-minute penalty is added for each missed target. The first athlete to finish the race is the winner. The men's individual event was added to the Olympics in 1980. The women's event first appeared in 1992.

SPRINT TO THE FINISH!

The biathlon sprint is a short version of the individual race. The men's sprint is 6.2 miles (10 km), and the women's is 4.7 miles (7.5 km). Each competitor skis the loop three times, stopping twice at the shooting range. Competitors must ski a 492-foot (150-m) penalty loop for each missed target. The men's sprint was added to the Olympics in 1980. The women's sprint made its **debut** in 1992.

HOT PURSUIT

To enter the men's 12.5km (7.8 mile) pursuit or the women's 10km (6.2 mile) pursuit, skiers must finish in the top 60 in the sprint events. In the pursuit, competitors ski five loops, stopping four times to shoot, with penalty loops for missed targets. A competitor who is **lapped** by another skier during the race must leave the competition.

FAIRY TALE HEROINE

Kati Wilhelm (GER) is nicknamed "Little Red Riding Hood" for her bright red hair and the bright red cap she wears while competing. She has won three biathlon golds, for the sprint and relay in 2002 and for the pursuit in 2006.

TURBO POWER

Uschi Disl (GER) was nicknamed "Turbo-disl" for earning nine biathlon medals over five different Olympic Games — more than any other woman! For her achievements, she was German Sportswoman of the Year in 2005.

READY, AIM, FIRE!

On the shooting ranges, the targets are five black circles on a white background. The targets are set back 164 feet (50 m). When a skier hits a target, the black circle falls, leaving a white space.

2006 OLYMPIC WOMEN'S MEDALISTS: 15km INDIVIDUAL: GOLD: SVETLANA ISHMOURATOVA (RUS)   SILVER: MARTINA GLAGOW (GER)   BRONZE: ALBINA AKHATOVA (RUS)
7.5km SPRINT: GOLD: FLORENCE BAVEREL-ROBERT (FRA)   SILVER: ANNA CARIN OLOFSSON (SWE)   BRONZE: LILIA EFREMOVA (UKR)
10km PURSUIT: GOLD: KATI WILHELM (GER)   SILVER: MARTINA GLAGOW (GER)   BRONZE: ALBINA AKHATOVA (RUS)

BIATHLON MASS START AND RELAYS

The men and women must scramble for the finish line
in the biathlon mass start and relay competitions.

*Germany's Uschi Disl (front) leads
the pack in the 2006 women's
12.5km biathlon mass start.*

2006 OLYMPIC MEN'S MEDALISTS: 15km MASS START: GOLD: MICHAEL GREIS (GER)
SILVER: TOMASZ SIKORA (POL)   BRONZE: OLE EINAR BJØRNDALEN (NOR)
4 x 7.5km RELAY: GOLD: GERMANY   SILVER: RUSSIA   BRONZE: FRANCE

ON YOUR MARK...

The men's 15km (9.3 mile) mass start and women's 12.5km (7.8 mile) mass start are new to the Olympics, since they debuted in 2006. Unlike events with an interval start, in the mass start, all the competitors line up at the starting line together and begin at the same time. They ski five loops, stopping four times to shoot, with a penalty loop for each missed target. A competitor who is lapped by another skier during the race must leave the competition.

Russian biathletes hand off during the 2006 women's 4 x 6km relay.

GO TEAM!

The biathlon relay has been part of the Olympics since 1968 for men and 1992 for women. The relay teams are made up of four skiers who must ski three times each and shoot twice. Each man skis 4.7 miles (7.5 km), and each woman skis 3.7 miles (6 km). To hand off, the incoming competitor pats the next skier on the back so she can continue the race. The winning team is the one whose final skier makes it across the finish line first.

DOUBLE GOLD

Frank-Peter Roetsch (GDR) was the first double-gold biathlon winner. Even though he missed three targets, he still won the individual 20km in 1988. He also won the 10km sprint at the same Olympics, despite a 492-foot (150-m) penalty loop!

BITE THE BULLET!

Relay competitors pack three extra bullets in case they miss any targets. After taking five regular shots, they must use the extra bullets to knock down any remaining targets. For every target that remains after the extra shots, competitors must ski a penalty loop.

TRIPLE CROWN PERFORMANCE

The first triple-gold medal biathlon winner was Michael Greis (GER). He won gold in three different events at the 2006 Olympics—the 20km individual, 15km mass start, and the relay.

2006 OLYMPIC WOMEN'S MEDALISTS: 12.5km MASS START: GOLD: ANNA CARIN OLOFSSON (SWE)   SILVER: KATI WILHELM (GER)   BRONZE: USCHI DISL (GER)   4 x 6km RELAY: GOLD: RUSSIA   SILVER: GERMANY   BRONZE: FRANCE

INTRODUCTION TO CROSS-COUNTRY SKIING

Cross-country skiing is not only the oldest skiing sport in the Olympics—it is the oldest form of skiing in the world. There are now six Olympic events—individual, individual sprint, pursuit, relay, team sprint, and mass start—for both men and women.

Bjorn Daehlie (NOR) earning one of his eight gold medals, in 1998.

DID YOU KNOW?

Only one U.S. athlete has ever won an Olympic medal in cross-country — Bill Koch, who won a silver in 1976.

ORIGINS

Paintings from thousands of years ago show hunters skiing after animals. More recently, the Swedish army was equipped with skis by the year 1500, and in the 1760s, the Norwegian army staged cross-country skiing races. Men began competing in cross-country in the Olympics in 1924, and women in 1952.

SLIDE, GLIDE, OR SKATE?

Cross-country skiers must use either the classic or free technique in different races. The specific technique for a particular race alternates between each Olympics. In some races, skiers are required to use one technique for part of the race and a different technique for the rest of the race.

SOLID GOLD

Bjorn Daehlie (NOR) has won the most gold medals of any athlete in Winter Olympic history, with eight. Over the course of his career, he competed in 15 cross-country races. He is the only athlete to win a total of 12 Olympic medals and the only one to win nine medals in individual events.

WINNING WAYS

Gunde Svan (SWE) has won a total of six Olympic medals in cross-country skiing, including four golds. In 1984, at age 22, he became the youngest athlete to win an Olympic cross-country race.

DISQUALIFIED!

Cross-country skiers can be **disqualified** for illegally using the wrong technique, such as using the free technique when the classic is required. Skiers can also be disqualified for getting in a competitor's way.

AN AMAZING CAREER

Raisa Smetanina (URS) is the only woman to win ten Olympic medals and the only person to win medals in five different Winter Games. She was 39 years old when she won her final medal — a gold in the relay in 1992. Smetanina was 23 years old when she competed in her first Olympics and 39 when she competed in her last.

Raisa Smetanina (URS), in action in 1988, winning one of her ten Winter Olympic medals.

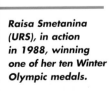

CROSS-COUNTRY: INDIVIDUAL AND INDIVIDUAL SPRINT

In cross-country races, the winner is the skier who crosses the finish line first — and the result can be a surprise!

Björn Lind (SWE) celebrates as he crosses the finish line in the 2006 cross-country individual sprint.

2006 OLYMPIC MEN'S MEDALISTS: 15km INDIVIDUAL: GOLD: ANDRUS VEERPALU (EST)
SILVER: LUKÁŠ BAUER (CZE)   BRONZE: TOBIAS ANGERER (GER)
INDIVIDUAL SPRINT: GOLD: BJÖRN LIND (SWE)   SILVER: RODDY DARRAGON (FRA)
BRONZE: THOBIAS FREDRIKSSON (SWE)

INDIVIDUAL CROSS-COUNTRY RACE

The men's individual race is 9.3 miles (15 km) long. The women's is 6.2 miles (10 km). In the 2010 Olympics, men and women will both use the free technique in this event. This race usually takes about 30 minutes to complete.

INDIVIDUAL SPRINT

The cross-country sprints are short races. The men's individual sprint race is 0.9 miles (1.4 km) long, while the women's is 0.7 miles (1.2 km). There are **qualifying rounds** to determine which men and women move on to the next rounds of competition, until the top six skiers race for the gold medal. The first one to cross the finish line wins.

STAGGERED START

The individual and individual sprint events use a **staggered start**, or interval method, to begin the race. One skier at a time leaves the starting gate, followed by the next skier about 30 seconds later.

BREAKING THE STREAK

During the 1956 Games, Pavel Kolchin (URS) won the bronze medal in the men's 15km event. He was the first athlete from a non-Scandinavian country to win an Olympic cross-country medal.

CLOSE CALL

In 1988, Marjo Matikainen (FIN) was in second place during most of the women's sprint event when she bolted ahead and won by only 1.3 seconds.

SURPRISE ENDING

Chandra Crawford (CAN) surprised her competitors when she surged ahead at the end of the women's individual sprint in 2006 to beat everyone for the gold. She used to compete in biathlon before switching sports.

Canada's Chandra Crawford (left), the surprise winner of the 2006 women's individual sprint.

2006 OLYMPIC WOMEN'S MEDALISTS: 10km INDIVIDUAL: GOLD: KRISTINA ŠMIGUN (EST)   SILVER: MARIT BJØRGEN (NOR)   BRONZE: HILDE GJERMUNDSHAUG PEDERSEN (NOR)
INDIVIDUAL SPRINT: GOLD: CHANDRA CRAWFORD (CAN)   SILVER: CLAUDIA KÜNZEL (GER)   BRONZE: ALENA SIDKO (RUS)

13

CROSS-COUNTRY: PURSUIT AND MASS START

In both the pursuit and mass start cross-country events, skiers begin the race with a mass start. The competitors leave the starting gate together, and the first one across the finish line wins.

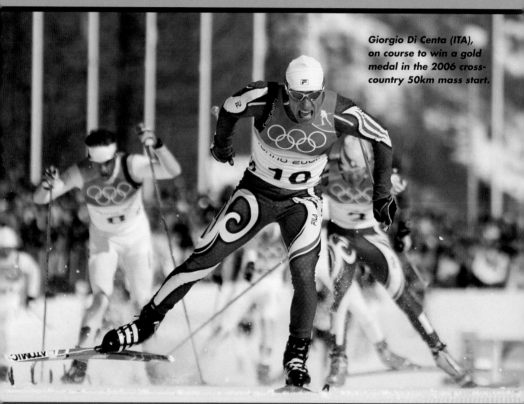

Giorgio Di Centa (ITA), on course to win a gold medal in the 2006 cross-country 50km mass start.

2006 OLYMPIC MEN'S MEDALISTS: 15 + 15km PURSUIT: GOLD: EUGENIY DEMENTIEV (RUS)
SILVER: FRODE ESTIL (NOR)   BRONZE: PIETRO PILLER COTTRER (ITA)
50km MASS START: GOLD: GIORGIO DI CENTA (ITA)   SILVER: EUGENIY DEMENTIEV (RUS)
BRONZE: MIKHAIL BOTVINOV (AUT)

SUPER STATS

In 2006, Giorgio Di Centa (ITA) beat Eugeniy Dementiev (RUS) in the men's mass start by only 0.8 seconds—the closest **margin of victory** in Olympic history. Dementiev did win gold, though, in the men's pursuit.

DID YOU KNOW?

Skiers use different skis and poles for classic and free skiing. The skis used for classic technique are longer than the skis used for free technique. The poles for free skiing are longer.

CROSS-COUNTRY PURSUIT

The men's pursuit begins with a 9.3-mile (15-km) leg done with the classic style, followed by a 9.3-mile (15-km) leg in the free style. The women's pursuit has two 4.7-mile (7.5-km) legs, one done in each style. Since 2006, the event has been done on one day. The men's race usually takes about 75 to 80 minutes, while the women's event usually takes about 45 minutes.

PRESTO, CHANGE-O!

Pursuit skiers have to change skis halfway through the race. They do this in a special area beside the course while the clock continues. Changing skis usually takes only about half a minute.

CROSS-COUNTRY MASS START

The mass start—which has been called a "ski marathon"—was introduced in 1992. Men ski 31 miles (50 km), and women ski 19 miles (30 km). The race usually takes about two hours for men and about $1\frac{1}{2}$ hours for women. The first skier to cross the finish line wins. Often, there are several skiers at the finish together, making this an exciting event to watch!

A FIRST FOR ESTONIA

In 2006, Kristina Šmigun (EST) became the first woman from her country to win a medal at the Winter Olympics when she captured gold in the pursuit. Four days after that performance, she added another gold when she beat Marit Bjørgen (NOR) in the women's individual race by only 21.3 seconds!

BETTER LATE THAN NEVER!

The first Canadian woman to win an Olympic medal in cross-country skiing was Beckie Scott. At first, she was awarded the bronze medal in 2002 for the women's pursuit. However, the athletes who finished first and second tested positive for **performance-enhancing drugs**, and their medals were taken back. Scott received her gold medal almost two years after the race!

2006 OLYMPIC WOMEN'S MEDALISTS: 7.5 + 7.5km PURSUIT: GOLD: KRISTINA ŠMIGUN (EST)
SILVER: KATERINA NEUMANNOVÁ (CZE)   BRONZE: EVGENIA MEDVEDEVA (RUS)
30km MASS START: GOLD: KATERINA NEUMANNOVÁ (CZE)
SILVER: JULIJA TCHEPALOVA (RUS)   BRONZE: JUSTYNA KOWALCZYK (POL)

15

CROSS-COUNTRY: RELAYS AND TEAM SPRINT

Cross-country can be a group event, too, as teammates scramble to make it across the finish line.

Cristian Zorzi crosses the finish line in triumph with an Italian flag at the end of the 2006 4 x 10km relay.

2006 OLYMPIC MEN'S MEDALISTS: 4 x 10km RELAY: GOLD: ITALY
SILVER: GERMANY   BRONZE: SWEDEN
TEAM SPRINT: GOLD: THOBIAS FREDRIKSSON & BJÖRN LIND (SWE)   SILVER: JENS ARNE
SVARTEDAL & TOR ARNE HETLAND (NOR)   BRONZE: IVAN ALYPOV & VASILI ROTCHEV (RUS

RELAY IT!

The men's 4 x 10km relay and the women's 4 x 5km relay require competitors to ski one lap, then exchange with another teammate. The four men on each team each ski one 6.2-mile (10-km) lap, while the four women on each team each ski one 2.5-mile (4-km) lap. The first two laps are done with classic technique, and the last two laps are done with free technique. The race begins with a mass start. Then, athletes change off to the next member of the team to ski with a pat on the back. A team wins when its anchor leg (the last person on the team to ski) crosses the finish line.

FIRST-TIME VICTORIES

Athletes from Finland won the first men's relay held, at the 1936 Olympics. Finland also won the first women's relay, in 1956.

TEAM SPRINT RACES

The team sprint is similar to the relay, but each team has only two skiers. The skiers alternate, each skiing the course three times. Each nation may enter only one team. The team sprint races are new to the Olympics and were first performed in 2006.

SWEET DEAL

When Sara Renner (CAN) broke her ski pole during the women's team sprint in 2006, the Norwegian coach, Bjørnar Håkensmoen, gave her another one to use. Renner continued on with the race, and she and Beckie Scott won the silver medal! To thank the coach, a Canadian businessman donated 8,000 cans of maple syrup to the Norwegian Olympic Committee.

DID YOU KNOW?

The first leg of the relay race is called the "scramble leg" because the athletes scramble to get in a good position after the mass start.

STREAKS SET AND BROKEN

When Italy won the 4 x 10km relay in 2006, it was their fifth straight medal in Winter Olympic cross-country relays. The bronze medal winning Swedish team captured their first relay medal since 1988, and Norway did not medal for the first time since that year.

ZORRO LEAVES HIS MARK!

At the 2006 Olympics, the Italian men's 4 x 10km relay team captured the gold medal. Their overall time was 30 seconds faster than the time set by Norway, the gold medal winners at the 2002 Olympics! The final team member, Cristian Zorzi (nicknamed "Zorro"), had enough time to grab an Italian flag from the crowd to wave as he crossed the finish line!

2006 OLYMPIC WOMEN'S MEDALISTS: 4 x 5km RELAY: GOLD: RUSSIA
SILVER: GERMANY   BRONZE: ITALY
TEAM SPRINT: GOLD: LINA ANDERSSON & ANNA DAHLBERG (SWE)   SILVER: SARA RENNER
& BECKIE SCOTT (CAN)   BRONZE: AINO KAISA SAARINEN & VIRPI KUITUNEN (FIN)

INTRODUCTION TO SKI JUMPING

Ski jumpers launch themselves off the mountain and into the air, soaring a distance the length of a football field—or longer—before they touch the ground.

Ski jumper Gregory Baxter (CAN) takes off, in 2006.

HISTORY

The first known ski jumper was a Norwegian army officer who put on a show for his fellow officers in 1809. Ski jumping became an Olympic sport in 1924 and has been in every Winter Olympics since then.

JUMP!

Ski jumpers launch themselves from a ramp at the end of a steep hill, soaring as far as possible before landing. Judges give competitors points for style, which are combined with the total distance of the jump for an overall score. Athletes must keep their skis steady, hold their balance, maintain body position, and land successfully. The athlete with the highest overall score wins!

OVER THE HILL

At the 2010 Olympics, ski jumping competitions will take place at Whistler Olympic Park. Athletes jump on the normal hill and the large hill.

GEAR UP

Ski jumpers use lightweight skis that are specifically designed for the sport. There are specific rules about their width, curve, and shape. Rules also exist about the suits worn by ski jumpers, which must be made of a spongy material with a specific thickness. Jumpers wear boots that are specially designed to let them lean forward while they are in the air. They also wear gloves, helmets, and goggles.

DID YOU KNOW?

So far, only men compete in ski jumping at the Olympics, but many people are working hard to see women's ski jumping become an Olympic event. The first World Championships in women's ski jumping took place in February 2009. The gold medal went to Lindsey Van (USA), who earned a total of 243 points for her two jumps. Silver went to Ulrike Graessler (GER), who had 239 points, and bronze to Anette Sagen (NOR), who ended up with 238.5 points.

LEARN THE LINGO

In-run—the part of the hill where jumpers gain speed as they approach the takeoff

Outrun—the flat section of the hill where jumpers slow down and stop after landing

Takeoff—the point where jumpers blast into the air from the end of a ramp to perform jumps

Matti Nykänen (FIN) in 1988, jumping in the old style with skis held parallel.

MORE ON SKI JUMPING

Ski jumpers compete both as individuals and as teams in one of the most spectacular winter sports.

2006 OLYMPIC MEDALISTS: INDIVIDUAL NH: GOLD: LARS BYSTØL (NOR)
SILVER: MATTI HAUTAMAKI (FIN) BRONZE: ROAR LJØKELSØY (NOR)

ON THEIR OWN

Jumpers get two jumps in individual NH (normal hill) and individual LH (large hill) competitions. The scores from the two jumps are added together to determine the winner.

GO TEAM!

The team event takes place on the large hill. Each team is made up of four skiers who jump twice. Their scores are added together to determine the winning team.

THE BEST

Matti Nykänen (FIN) is considered the best ski jumper in history with five Olympic medals. He also won all three events in ski jumping at the 1988 Olympics! His countryman, Toni Nieminen, won three medals for ski jumping at the 1992 Olympics — two golds and a bronze. Amazingly, it was his first time at the Olympics!

FLYING V

Ski jumpers used to jump with their skis held parallel to each other. In the 1980s, a new style developed, where jumpers held their skis in a V shape, with the tips spread apart. Today, almost all skiers use the V-style because it is more **aerodynamic** and produces longer jumps.

Austria's Thomas Morgenstern, celebrating after his team won gold in 2006.

HOMETOWN HERO

Ski jumper Yukio Kasaya (JPN) won Japan's first gold medal at a Winter Olympics in 1972. In fact, Japanese athletes won all three medals that year in the individual NH event — in Japan!

TIMELESS

Imagine receiving a medal 50 years late! That's what happened to Anders Haugen (USA) when it was discovered that an error had been made in the scoring at the 1924 Olympics.

2006 OLYMPIC MEDALISTS: INDIVIDUAL LH: GOLD: THOMAS MORGENSTERN (AUT) SILVER: ANDREAS KOFLER (AUT) BRONZE: LARS BYSTØL (NOR) TEAM LH: GOLD: AUSTRIA SILVER: FINLAND BRONZE: NORWAY

21

INTRODUCTION TO NORDIC COMBINED

What do you get when you mix cross-country skiing with ski jumping? Nordic combined!

Felix Gottwald (AUT), in the ski jumping portion of the 2006 Nordic combined.

SUPER STATS

Norway holds the record for most medals awarded in Nordic combined with 26 — 11 gold, eight silver, and seven bronze. Germany is next, with 17, followed by Finland, with 13.

DID YOU KNOW?

• The time between the ski jumping competition and the cross-country race can be as little as 35 minutes or as long as several hours.

• Free technique is used during the cross-country skiing portion of the Nordic combined.

A TRIO OF EVENTS

Only men compete in Nordic combined. There are three events:
• Individual NH/10km — a jump off the normal hill, plus a 10km (6.2 mile) cross-country race
• Individual LH/10km — a jump off the large hill, plus a 10km cross-country race
• Team LH/4 x 5km — a team of four, with each member jumping once off the large hill, followed by a cross-country relay race in which each member skis a 5km (3.1 mile) leg

OLYMPIC HISTORY

The individual Nordic combined has been part of the Olympics since 1924. The team event was added in 1988.

NEW RULES

The format of the Nordic combined has changed over the years. Competition in an event used to be held over two days and included two jumps. Now, in the individual events, competitors perform only one jump, and competition takes place on a single day. The athlete with the highest score in ski jumping starts first in cross-country. The first athlete across the finish line wins.

MASTER OF THE SLOPES

The first athlete to win a gold medal in Nordic combined was Thorleif Haug (NOR), in 1924. He also won two gold medals in cross-country skiing at the same Olympics.

PUT IT IN REVERSE

Before the 1950s, the cross-country portion of the Nordic combined was held before the ski jumping competition. However, athletes in the lead after the skiing portion had such high scores that they almost always won. By reversing the competition order, the final result became more unpredictable — as well as more exciting for spectators to watch!

NORDIC COMBINED: INDIVIDUAL EVENTS

Competitors in Nordic combined must show technical skill as well as endurance and strength.

Takanori Kono (JPN), helping his team win the Nordic combined team event in 1994.

2006 OLYMPIC MEDALISTS: INDIVIDUAL NH/10km: GOLD: GEORG HETTICH (GER)
SILVER: FELIX GOTTWALD (AUT)   BRONZE: MAGNUS MOAN (NOR)

CHANGING DISTANCES

The format for the individual LH event has been changed since the 2006 Olympics. The cross-country part used to be a 4.7-mile (7.5-km) sprint, but in the 2010 Olympics, it will be longer, at 6.2 miles (10 km).

SMOOTH LANDING

In order to complete a ski jump correctly, the landing must be in **Telemark** stance. This landing position requires the athlete to lunge, putting one leg slightly ahead of the other upon landing, with both skis pointing forward. Style marks are deducted if the athlete does not perform the Telemark landing.

CONSISTENT PERFORMANCE

Ulrich Wehling (GDR) won the Nordic combined three times — in 1972, 1976, and 1980. He was the first man to win three Winter Olympic gold medals for the same individual event at three **consecutive** Olympics.

SILVER LINING

Takanori Kono (JPN) received a silver medal in the individual Nordic combined in 1994 — the only Japanese athlete ever to win an individual medal in the sport. Japan, however, did win the team event twice, in 1992 and 1994. Kono was a member of both of these medal winning teams.

BROKEN PATTERN

From 1924 to 1936, Norwegian athletes won every Olympic Nordic combined medal. Heikki Hasu (FIN) was the first non-Norwegian skier to win the Nordic combined, in 1948 — a year in which Norway was shut out. At the 1952 Games, though, Norway was back on the **podium** with gold and bronze!

Georg Hettich (GER) crosses the finish line in the 2006 7.5km sprint.

2006 OLYMPIC MEDALISTS: INDIVIDUAL LH/7.5km: GOLD: FELIX GOTTWALD (AUT)
SILVER: MAGNUS MOAN (NOR)   BRONZE: GEORG HETTICH (GER)

25

NORDIC COMBINED: TEAM EVENT

When the Nordic combined team event was introduced to the Olympics in 1988, teams had only three skiers. Since 1998, four men have teamed up to try to win the gold.

A victory celebration by the Austrian team that won the gold medal in the 2006 Nordic combined relay event.

2006 OLYMPIC MEDALISTS: **TEAM LH/4 x 5km:**   **GOLD: AUSTRIA**

RACE BASICS

In the team competition, each member performs one jump on the large hill. The team with the highest combined score starts first in the cross-country relay race. Each member skis a 3.1-mile (5-km) leg. The first team with all four members across the finish line wins.

WAX ON, WAX OFF!

In order to glide over the snow easily, skiers apply a type of wax called glide wax to the bottom of their skis. If they are skiing with the classic style, athletes apply wax only to the front and rear tips of the skis. Free technique requires wax on the entire bottom surface of the skis.

GOTCHA!

Felix Gottwald (AUT) began competing in the Olympics when he was only 18. He won a total of six medals (two gold, a silver, and three bronze) in three Nordic combined events over the course of two Olympics—2002 and 2006— including a gold and bronze in the team competition.

DELAYED

At the 2006 Olympics, high winds on the ski jumping hill forced officials to delay a portion of that part of the competition. Midway through the ski jumping, the competition was stopped. It was completed the next day.

PRODIGY

Samppa Lajunen (FIN) won the overall World title in Nordic combined in 1997, when he was only 17. He continued his winning ways the next year at the Olympics, at age 18, when he won two silvers, one in the team event and one in an individual event. Things got even better for him in 2002, when he won three golds, taking two individual competitions and leading his team to victory as well.

DID YOU KNOW?

- *Skiers may use any skiing technique—classic or free—in the relay portion of the Nordic combined.*

- *The same four competitors from each team must complete both portions of the event. There are no substitutions allowed.*

- *Ski jumping is held in the morning, followed by cross-country in the afternoon.*

IN THE MEDALS

Since 1998, Japan has won the Nordic combined team event twice at the Olympics. The other winners have been West Germany, Norway, Finland, and Austria.

FULL SET

Georg Hettich (GER) won a full set of medals at the 2006 Olympic Games in Nordic combined. He took gold in the individual NH/10km event, silver in the team LH/4 x 5km event, and bronze in the individual LH/7.5km sprint.

A SNAPSHOT OF THE VANCOUVER 2010 WINTER OLYMPICS

BIATHLON, CROSS-COUNTRY, SKI JUMPING, AND NORDIC COMBINED
THE ATHLETES

Everyone is getting ready for Vancouver in 2010! Olympic teams are still being determined. The listings below include the top finishers in a selection of events in the 2009 World Championships. Who among them will be the athletes to watch in the Vancouver Winter Olympics? Visit the Web site www.vancouver2010.com for more information about the upcoming competitions.

BIATHLON EVENTS

Men—10km sprint:
1. Ole Einer Bjøerndalen (NOR)
2. Dmitri Yaroshenko (RUS)
3. Emil Hegle Svendsen (NOR)

Men—12.5km pursuit:
1. Ole Einer Bjøerndalen (NOR)
2. Tomasz Sikora (POL)
3. Emil Hegle Svendsen (NOR)

Men—15km mass start:
1. Ole Einer Bjøerndalen (NOR)
2. Tomasz Sikora (POL)
3. Emil Hegle Svendsen (NOR)

Women—7.5km sprint:
1. Helena Jonsson (SWE)
2. Kati Wilhelm (GER)
3. Magdalena Neuner (GER)

Women—10km pursuit:
1. Helena Jonsson (SWE)
2. Kati Wilhelm (GER)
3. Magdalena Neuner (GER)

Women—12.5km mass start:
1. Helena Jonsson (SWE)
2. Kati Wilhelm (GER)
3. Tora Berger (NOR)

Norwegian biathlete Emil Hegle Svendsen competes during the 12.5 km pursuit race at the Biathlon World Cup in Ruhpolding, Germany, January 18, 2009.

CROSS-COUNTRY SKIING EVENTS

2009 FIS Nordic World Ski Championships

Men—Individual sprint freestyle:
1. Ola Vigen Hattestad (NOR)
2. Johan Kjolstad (NOR)
3. Nikolay Morilov (RUS)

Men—Team sprint classical:
1. Ola Vigen Hattestad, Johan Kjolstad (NOR)
2. Axel Teichmann, Tobias Angerer (GER)
3. Sami Jauhojarvi, Ville Nousiainen (FIN)

Women—Individual sprint freestyle:
1. Arianna Follis (ITA)
2. Kikkan Randall (USA)
3. Pirjo Muranen (FIN)

Women—Team sprint classical:
1. Aino-Kaisa Saarinen, Virpi Kuitunen (FIN)
2. Lina Andersson, Anna Olsson (SWE)
3. Marianna Ionga, Arianna Follis (ITA)

SKI JUMPING EVENTS

2009 World Championships

Men—Individual normal hill:
1. Wolfgang Loitzl (AUT)
2. Gregor Schlierenzauer (AUT)
3. Simon Ammann (SUI)

Men—Individual large hill:
1. Andreas Kuttel (SUI)
2. Martin Schmitt (GER)
3. Anders Jacobsen (NOR)

Men—Team large hill:
1. Austria
2. Norway
3. Japan

Women—Individual normal hill:
1. Lindsey Van (USA)
2. Ulrike Grassler (GER)
3. Anette Sagen (NOR)

NORDIC COMBINED EVENTS

2009 World Championships

Men—10km individual normal hill:
1. Todd Lodwick (USA)
2. Jan Schmid (NOR)
3. Bill Demong (USA)

Men—10km individual large hill:
1. Bill Demong (USA)
2. Bjorn Kircheisen (GER)
3. Jason Lamy Chappius (FRA)

Men—10km mass start:
1. Todd Lodwick (USA)
2. Tino Edelmann (GER)
3. Jason Lamy Chappius (FRA)

Men—4x5 km freestyle team:
1. Japan
2. Germany
3. Norway

THE VENUE IN VANCOUVER
WHISTLER OLYMPIC/ PARALYMPIC PARK

- venue capacity: 12,000 in each of three stadiums
- located in Whistler, British Columbia
- one-square-kilometre (0.6 square miles) includes three separate stadiums for cross-country skiing, biathlon, and ski jumping
- stadiums are located about one quarter mile (400 m) apart
- biathlon stadium has 30 lanes
- approximately 9.3 miles (15 km) of trails for cross-country skiing and biathlon
- an electronic target system records the precise time and hit or miss of each bullet fired
- two ski jumps (normal hill and large hill) include one of the world's most complex snow refrigeration and track setting systems

GLOSSARY

aerodynamic Designed to move without being blocked by the wind

consecutive Happening in order, one after another

debut To perform something for the first time or the first time an event is added to competition

disqualified To be eliminated from competition for not following the rules

endurance The ability to keep at a difficult activity for a long time

interval A set amount of time between two happenings

lapped When a competitor is overtaken and passed by another competitor in a race by the full distance of a lap

margin of victory The difference in time or score between a first-place finish and the second-place finish

mass start A race format in which several athletes begin at once.

parallel Referring to lines that are always the same distance apart and never meet

penalty In sports, a punishment for missing a shot or failing at something

performance-enhancing drug A substance used by athletes to improve their ability to perform a sport, which is against the rules

podium A platform on which the winners of an event stand

prone position Lying down flat on the stomach; one of the postures taken for shooting targets in biathlon

qualifying round A stage of competition that competitors must succeed at in order to move on to the next stage

relay A type of race in which teams compete, with each member of the team going part of the distance

Scandinavian Referring to several northern European countries including Norway, Denmark, Sweden, Iceland, and Finland

staggered start Beginning a competition with participants starting one at a time at regular intervals

standing position Standing upright; one of the postures taken for shooting targets in biathlon

Telemark A landing position in ski jumping, in which the athlete lunges with one leg slightly ahead of the other and both skis pointed forward

FIND OUT MORE

BOOKS

Herran, Joe, and Ron Thomas. *Skiing* (Philadelphia: Chelsea House, 2007)

Hindman, Steve. *Cross-Country Skiing: Building Skills for Fun and Fitness* (Seattle: Mountaineers Books, 2005)

Judd, Ron C. *The Winter Olympics: An Insider's Guide to the Legends, the Lore, and the Games* (Seattle: Mountaineers Books, 2009)

Macy, Sue. *Freezeframe: A Photographic History of the Winter Olympics* (Washington, DC: National Geographic Children's Books, 2006)

Wallechinsky, David, and Jamie Loucky. *The Complete Book of the Winter Olympics, Turin 2006 Edition* (Toronto: SportClassic Books, 2005)

WEB SITES

Canadian Olympic Committee   www.olympic.ca
The official site of the Canadian Olympic Committee, with information on athletes, sports, and the Olympics.

International Biathlon Union   www.biathlonworld.com
Biathlon competitions, techniques, and more.

International Olympic Committee   www.olympic.org
The official site of the International Olympic Committee, with information on all Olympic sports.

International Ski Federation   www.fis-ski.com
The official site of the organization, made up of more than 100 national ski federations, overseeing all types of competitive skiing.

Ski Jumping USA   www.skijumpingcentral.com
All about the sport of ski jumping.

U.S. Olympic Committee   www.usoc.org/
The official site of the U.S. Olympic Committee, with information on athletes, sports, and the Olympics.

U.S. Ski Team   www.usskiteam.com
The official site of the U.S. teams in all types of skiing.

INDEX

COUNTRY ABBREVIATIONS

AUT — Austria
CAN — Canada
CZE — Czechoslovakia/ Czech Republic
EST — Estonia
FIN — Finland
FRA — France
GDR — East Germany (1949–1990)
GER — Germany
ITA — Italy
JPN — Japan
NOR — Norway
POL — Poland
RUS — Russia
SWE — Sweden
UKR — Ukraine
URS — Soviet Union (1922–1992)
USA — United States of America

Printed in the U.S.A. — CG